Illustrations by Paul Hess

Text by JoAnn Early Macken

Gareth Stevens Publishing
A WORLD ALMANAC EDUCATION GROUP COMPANY

Please visit our web site at: www.garethstevens.com
For a free color catalog describing Gareth Stevens Publishing's
list of high-quality books and multimedia programs,
call 1-800-542-2595 or fax your request to (414) 332-3567.

For Karen Scawen — P. H.
For The Hive, my classmates in the Vermont College MFA in Writing for Children Program — J. E. M.

Library of Congress Cataloging-in-Publication Data

Macken, JoAnn Early.
    Farm animals / text by JoAnn Early Macken; illustrations by Paul Hess.
       p. cm. — (Animal worlds)
    Includes bibliographical references.
    Summary: Simple text and illustrations introduce various animals that live on farms.
    ISBN 0-8368-3039-3 (lib. bdg.)
    1. Domestic animals—Juvenile literature. [1. Domestic animals.] I. Hess, Paul, ill.
  II. Title.
  SF75.5.M34   2002
  636—dc21   2001054159

This North American edition first published in 2002 by
Gareth Stevens Publishing
A World Almanac Education Group Company
330 West Olive Street, Suite 100
Milwaukee, Wisconsin 53212 USA

Book design: Sarah Godwin
Gareth Stevens cover design: Katherine A. Goedheer
Gareth Stevens series editor: Dorothy L. Gibbs

Printed in the United States of America

1 2 3 4 5 6 7 8 9 06 05 04 03 02

Table of Contents

Farms

Long ago, farms did not have very many animals. Most of the animals were raised for food. Others pulled the plows. Today, some farms keep huge herds of cattle or lots of pigs, horses, sheep, or chickens. Now, machines do most of the work. Some farms raise worms, fish, or ostriches. Others only grow crops.

Sheep

Sheep can climb over rough, rocky ground. They grow thick coats of wool, called fleece, for winter. Their wool can be short and curly or long and shaggy.

Rooster

Roosters are grown-up male chickens. They are known for their crowing and can wake people up. The crests on their heads are called combs.

Cow

Cows stay together in herds. When the weather is warm, they eat grass in a field. They follow each other in a line to be milked.

Horse

Horses can run far and fast and jump high. On farms, they haul heavy loads. They eat oats and hay. Carrots and apples are special treats.

Goat

Goats climb up high to get a good view. They stand on their back legs to eat the bark and leaves of trees. Male goats usually have a beard.

Pig

Pigs can be black, white, tan, or pink. Some are spotted. All pigs have curly tails. Pigs are the smartest farm animals.

Goose

A goose is bigger than a duck but smaller than a swan. Geese honk or cackle. Their webbed feet make them good swimmers. They fly fast, too.

Dog

Dogs know people and things by their sounds and smells. A happy dog wags its tail. A woof can be a warning. All dogs are related to wolves.